Things That Can and Cannot Be Said

OCT 4 - 2016

Things That Can and Cannot Be Said
Essays and Conversations

Arundhati Roy and John Cusack

Haymarket Books
Chicago, Illinois

Published in 2016 by
Haymarket Books
P.O. Box 180165
Chicago, IL 60618
773-583-7884
www.haymarketbooks.org
info@haymarketbooks.org

ISBN: 978-1-60846-717-4

Trade distribution:
In the US, Consortium Book Sales and Distribution, www.cbsd.com
In Canada, Publishers Group Canada, www.pgcbooks.ca

This book was published with the generous support of Wallace Action
Fund and Lannan Foundation.

Cover and interior design by Ragina Johnson. Cover image of the National
Geospatial-Intelligence Agency; Springfield, Virginia, courtesy Trevor
Paglen; Metro Pictures, New York; Altman Siegel, San Francisco

Photo Credits
p. 8: photo by Ole von Uexküll, used by permission of the photographer;
p. 30: August 6, 1963, AP photo by Horst Faas; p. 34: November 1967, AP
photo; p. 46: photo by Arundhati Roy; p. 49: Photo by John Cusack; p. 56:
Map from Palestinian Academic Society for the Study of International
Affairs, www.passia.org; p. 64: AP photo by Ajit Solanki; p. 68: photo
by John Cusack; p. 70: photo by Ole von Uexküll; pp. 74–75: photo by
Arundhati Roy; p. 80: photo by Ole von Uexküll

Conversations transcribed by Katherine Smith.

Printed in Canada by union labor.

Library of Congress Cataloging-in-Publication data is available.

10 9 8 7 6 5 4 3 2 1

RECYCLED
Paper made from
recycled material
FSC® C103567

John Cusack

Things That Can and Cannot Be Said

"Every nation-state, by supposition, tends toward the imperial: that is the point. Through banks, armies, secret police, propaganda, courts and jails, treaties, treasuries, taxes, laws and orders, myths of civil obedience, assumptions of civic virtue at the top...

Still it should be said that of the political left, we expect something better. And correctly. We put more trust in those who show a measure of compassion. We agree, conditionally but instinctively, with those who denounce the hideous social arrangements which make war inevitable and human want omnipresent; which foster corporate selfishness, pander to appetites and disorder, waste the earth."

—**Daniel Berrigan**, from *The Nightmare of God: The Book of Revelation*, 1983

One morning as I scanned the news—horror in the Middle East, Russia and America facing off in Ukraine—I thought of Edward Snowden and wondered how he was holding up in Moscow. I began to imagine a conversation between him and Daniel Ellsberg (who leaked the Pentagon Papers during the Vietnam War). And then, interestingly, in my imagination a third person made her way into the room—the writer Arundhati Roy. It occurred to me that trying to get the three of them together would be a fine thing to do.

I had heard Roy speak in Chicago, and had met her several times.[1] One gets the feeling very quickly and comes to the rapid conclusion that with her there are no preformatted assumptions or givens. Through our conversations I became very aware that what gets lost, or goes unsaid, in most of the debates around surveillance and whistleblowing is a perspective and context from outside the United States and Europe. The debates around them have gradually centered on corporate overreach and the privacy rights of US citizens.

The philosopher/theosophist Rudolf Steiner says that any perception or truth that is isolated and removed from its larger context ceases to be true:

> When any single thought emerges in consciousness, I cannot rest until this is brought into

harmony with the remainder. Such an isolated concept is entirely unendurable. I am simply conscious that there exists an inwardly sustained harmony among all thoughts. . . . Therefore every such isolation is an abnormality, an untruth. When we have arrived at that state of mind in which our whole thought world bears the character of complete inner harmony, we gain thereby the satisfaction for which our mind is striving. We feel that we are in possession of the truth.[2]

In other words, every isolated idea that doesn't relate to others yet is taken as true (as a kind of niche truth) is not just bad politics, it is somehow also fundamentally untrue . . . To me, Arundhati Roy's writing and thinking strives for such unity of thought. And for her, like for Steiner, reason comes from the heart.

I knew Dan and Ed because we all worked together on the Freedom of the Press Foundation.[3] And I knew Roy admired both of them greatly, but she was disconcerted by the photograph of Ed cradling the American flag in his arms that had appeared on the cover of *Wired*.[4] On the other hand, she was impressed by what he had said in the interview—in particular that one of the factors that pushed him into doing what he did was the NSA (National Security Agency)'s sharing real-time data of Palestinians in the United States with the Israeli

ACT / SEP 2014

government. She thought what Dan and Ed had done were tremendous acts of courage, though as far as I could tell, her own politics were more in sync with Julian Assange's. "Snowden is the thoughtful, courageous saint of liberal reform," she once said to me. "And Julian Assange is a sort of radical, feral prophet who has been prowling this wilderness since he was sixteen years old."

I had recorded many of our conversations, Roy's and mine—for no reason other than that they were so intense that I felt I needed to listen to them several times over to understand what we were really saying to each other. She didn't seem to notice, or if she did, she didn't seem to mind. When I asked her if I could use some of the transcripts, she said, "Okay, but make sure you edit out the idiocy. At least mine."

I'll roll the tapes:

AR: All I'm saying is: what does that American flag mean to people outside of America? What does it mean in Afghanistan, Iraq, Iran, Palestine, Pakistan—even in India, your new "natural ally"?[5]

JC: In his [Ed's] situation, he's got very little margin for error when it comes to controlling his image, his messaging, and he's done an incredible job up to this point.

But you're troubled by that isolated iconography?

AR: Forget the genocide of American Indians, forget slavery, forget Hiroshima, forget Cambodia, forget Vietnam, you know ...

JC: Why do we have to forget?

(*Laughter*)

AR: I'm just saying that, at one level, I am happy— awed—that there are people of such intelligence, such compassion, that have defected from the state. They are heroic. Absolutely. They've risked their lives, their free- dom ... but then there's that part of me that thinks ... How could you ever have believed in it? What do you feel betrayed by? Is it possible to have a moral state? A moral superpower? I can't understand those people who believe that the excesses are just aberrations.... Of course, I understand it intellectually, but ... part of me wants to retain that incomprehension. . . . Sometimes my anger gets in the way of their pain.

JC: Fair enough, but don't you think you're being a little harsh?

AR: Maybe (*laughs*). But then, having ranted as I have, I always say that the grand thing in the United States is that there has been real resistance from within. There have been soldiers who've refused to fight, who've burned their medals, who've been conscientious objectors.[6] I don't think we have ever had a conscientious objector in the Indian Army. Not one. In the United States, you have this proud history, you know? And Snowden is part of that.

JC: My gut tells me Snowden is more radical than he lets on. He has to be so tactical . . .

AR: Just since 9/11 . . . we're supposed to forget whatever happened in the past because 9/11 is where history begins. Okay, since 2001, how many wars have been started, how many countries have been destroyed? So now ISIS [also known as Islamic State in Iraq and al-Sham] is the new evil—but how did that evil begin? Is it more evil to do what ISIS is doing, which is to go around massacring people—mainly, but not only, Shi'a—slitting throats? By the way, the US-backed militias are doing similar things, except they don't show beheadings of white folks on TV. Or is it more evil to contaminate the water supply, to bomb a place with depleted uranium, to cut off the supply of medicines, to say that half a million children dying from economic sanctions is a "hard price," but "worth it"?[7]

JC: Madeleine Albright said so—about Iraq.

"In Syria, you're on the side of those who want to depose Assad, right? And then suddenly, you're with Assad, wanting to fight ISIS. It's like some crazed, bewildered, rich giant bumbling around in a poor area with his pockets stuffed with money, and lots of weapons—just throwing stuff around."

AR: Yes. Iraq. Is it alright to force a country to disarm, and then bomb it? To continue to create mayhem in the area? To pretend that you are fighting radical Islamism, when you're actually toppling all the regimes that are not radical Islamist regimes? Whatever else their faults may be, they were not radical Islamist states—Iraq was not, Syria is not, Libya was not. The most radical fundamentalist Islamist state is, of course, your ally Saudi Arabia. In Syria, you're on the side of those who want to depose Assad, right? And then suddenly, you're with Assad, wanting to fight ISIS. It's like some crazed, bewildered, rich giant bumbling around in a poor area with his pockets stuffed with money, and lots of weapons—just throwing stuff around. You don't even really know who you're giving it to—which murderous faction you are arming against which—feeling very relevant when actually . . . All this destruction that has come in the wake of 9/11, all the countries that have been bombed . . . it ignites and magnifies these ancient antagonisms. They don't necessarily have to do with the United States; they predate the existence of the United States by centuries. But the United States is unable to understand how irrelevant it is, actually. And how wicked . . . Your short-term gains are the rest of the world's long-term disasters—for everybody, including yourselves.[8] And, I'm sorry, I've been saying *you* and *the United States* or *America,* when I actually mean the US government. There's a difference. Big one.

JC: Yeah.

AR: Conflating the two the way I just did is stupid . . . walking into a trap—it makes it easy for people to say, "Oh, she's anti-American, he's anti-American," when we're not. Of course not. There are things I love about America. Anyway, what is a country? When people say, "Tell me about India," I say, "Which India? . . . The land of poetry and mad rebellion? The one that produces haunting music and exquisite textiles? The one that invented the caste system and celebrates the genocide of Muslims and Sikhs and the lynching of Dalits? The country of dollar billionaires? Or the one in which 800 million live on less than half a dollar a day?[9] Which India?" When people say "America," which one? Bob Dylan's or Barack Obama's? New Orleans or New York? Just a few years ago India, Pakistan, and Bangladesh were one country. Actually, we were many countries if you count the princely states. . . . Then the British drew a line, and now we're three countries, two of them pointing nukes at each other—the radical Hindu bomb and the radical Muslim bomb.[10]

JC: Radical Islam and US exceptionalism are in bed with each other. They're like lovers, methinks . . .

AR: It's a revolving bed in a cheap motel . . . Radical Hinduism is snuggled up somewhere in there, too. It's

"Radical Islam and US exceptionalism
are in bed with each other.
They're like lovers, methinks . . ."

hard to keep track of the partners; they change so fast. Each new baby they make is the latest progeny of the means to wage eternal war.

JC: If you help manufacture an enemy that's *really* evil, you can point to the fact that it's really evil, and say, "Hey, it's *really* evil."

AR: Your enemies are always manufactured to suit your purpose, right? How can you have a good enemy? You have to have an utterly evil enemy—and then the evilness has to progress.

JC: It has to metastasize, right?

AR: Yes. And then . . . how often are we going to keep on saying the same things?

JC: Yeah, you get worn out by it.

AR: Truly, there's no alternative to stupidity. Cretinism is the mother of fascism. I have no defense against it, really . . .

JC: It's a real problem.

(*Both laugh*)

AR: It isn't the lies they tell, it's the *quality* of the lies that becomes so humiliating. They've stopped caring about even that. It's all a play. Hiroshima and Nagasaki happen, there are hundreds of thousands of dead, and the curtain comes down, and that's the end of that. Then Korea happens. Vietnam happens, all that happened in Latin America happens. And every now and then, this curtain comes down and history begins anew. New moralities and new indignations are manufactured . . . in a disappeared history.

JC: And a disappeared context.

AR: Yes, without any context or memory. But the people of the world have memories. There was a time when the women of Afghanistan—at least in Kabul— were out there. They were allowed to study; they were doctors and surgeons, walking free, wearing what they wanted. That was when it was under Soviet occupation. Then the United States starts funding the mujahideen. Reagan called them Afghanistan's "founding fathers."[11] It reincarnates the idea of "jihad," virtually creates the Taliban. And what happens to the women? In Iraq, until before the war, the women were scientists, museum directors, doctors. I'm not valorizing Saddam Hussein or the Soviet occupation of Afghanistan, which was brutal and killed hundreds of thousands of people—it was the Soviet Union's Vietnam. I'm just saying that now, in these new wars, whole countries have slipped into mayhem—the women have just been pushed back into their burqas—and not by choice. I mean, to me, one thing is a culture in which women have not broken out of their subservience, but the horror of tomorrow, somebody turning around and telling me: "Arundhati, just go back into your veil, and sit in your kitchen and don't come out." Can you imagine the violence of that? That's what has happened to these women. In 2001, we were told that the war in Afghanistan was a feminist mission. The marines were liberating Afghan women from the Taliban.[12] Can you really bomb feminism into a country? And now, after twenty-five years of brutal war—ten years against the Soviet occupation, fifteen years of US occupation—the Taliban is riding back to Kabul and will soon be back to doing business with the United States. I don't live in the United States, but when I'm here, I begin to feel like my head is in a grinder—my brains are being scrambled by this language that they're using. Outside [the United States] it's not so hard to understand because people know the score. But here, so many seem to swallow the propaganda so obediently.

So that was one exchange. Here's another:

JC: So, what do you think? What do we think are the things we can't talk about in a civilized society, if you're a good, domesticated house pet?

AR: (*Laughs*) The occasional immorality of preaching nonviolence?

(This was a reference to *Walking with the Comrades*, Roy's account of her time spent in the forests of central India with armed guerrillas who were fighting paramilitary forces and vigilante militias trying to clear indigenous people off their land, which had been handed over to mining companies.[13])

JC: In the United States, we can talk about ISIS, but we can't talk about Palestine.

AR: Oh, in India, we can talk about Palestine, but we can't talk about Kashmir.[14] Nowadays, we can't talk about the daylight massacre of thousands of Muslims in Gujarat, because Narendra Modi might become prime minister.[15] [As he did subsequently in May 2014.] They like to say, "Let bygones be bygones." *Bygones*. Nice word . . . old-fashioned.

JC: Sounds like a sweet goodbye.

AR: And we can decide the most convenient place on which to airdrop history's markers. History is really a study of the future, not the past.

JC: I just want to know what I can't talk about, so I'll avoid it in social settings.

AR: You can say, for example, that it's wrong to behead people physically, like with a knife, which implies that it's alright to blow their heads off with a drone... isn't it?

JC: Well, a drone is so surgical ... and it's like, a quick thing. They don't suffer, right?

AR: But some "muzzlims," as you call them, are also good, professional butchers. They do it quick.

JC: What else can and cannot be said?

AR: This is a lovely theme ... About Vietnam, you can say, "These Asians, they don't value their lives, and so they force us to bear the burden of genocide." This is more or less a direct quote.

JC: From William Westmoreland.[16]

AR: Yes, there was Westmoreland and then there was Saint Robert McNamara, who supervised the destruction in Vietnam and also planned the bombing of Tokyo, in which more than eighty thousand people were killed in a single night.[17] Then he became the president of the World Bank, where he took great care of the world's poor. At the end of his life, he was tormented by one question—"How much evil must we do in order to do good?" That's a quote, too.[18]

JC: It's tough love.

AR: Fucking selfless stuff ...

We had these conversations sitting at my kitchen table, in New York corner booths, in a Puerto Rican diner that became a favorite spot. On impulse, I called New Delhi.

Wanna go to Moscow and meet Dan Ellsberg and Ed Snowden?

Don't talk rubbish ...

Listen ... if I can pull it off, should we go?

There was silence, and I felt the smile over the phone.

Yaa, Maan. Let's go.

[War] culminates in a kind of last ditch moral nightmare. People begin worshipping a mysterious slouching beast, following after, bowing down, offering gifts, making much of zero; and worse. Love of death, idolatry, fear of life; that roughshod trek of war and warmakers through the world, hand in hand with death. Long live death!

They wouldn't worship if they weren't in love. Or if they weren't in fear. The second being a state as devouring, at least, as the first. I think the clue is the second, masquerading as the first. Just as the beast is the ape of God; to do some things successfully, you have above all to hide what you're up to. In this way fear can ape love, death can demand a tribute owed to life, the ape can play God.

Such reflections are of course ill received by some: those to whom the state is a given, the Church a given, Western culture a given, war a given; likewise consumerism, taxpaying.

All the neat slots of existence into which one is to fit, birth to death and every point between. Nothing to be created, no one to be responsible to, nothing to risk, no objections to lodge. . . . Life is a mechanical horizontal sidewalk, of the kind you sometimes ride at airports between buildings. One is carried along, a zonked spectator. . . .

Every nation-state, by supposition, tends toward the imperial: that is the point. Through banks, armies, secret police, propaganda, courts and jails, treaties, treasuries, taxes, laws and orders, myths of civil obedience, assumptions of civic virtue at the top. Revelation in fact urges on us, in response to all this, a kind of Christian scepticism, in face of every political form and promise.

Still it should be said that of the political left, we expect something better. And correctly. We put more trust in those who show a measure of compassion. We agree, conditionally but instinctively, with those who denounce the hideous social arrangements which make war inevitable and human want omnipresent; which foster corporate selfishness, pander to appetites and disorder, waste the earth.

—**Daniel Berrigan**, from *The Nightmare of God: The Book of Revelation*, 1983

Arundhati Roy

"We Brought You the Promise of the Future, but Our Tongue Stammered and Barked…"

My phone rang at three in the morning. It was John Cusack asking me if I would go with him to Moscow to meet Edward Snowden. I'd met John several times; I'd walked the streets of Chicago with him, a hulking fellow hunched into his black hoodie, trying not to be recognized. I'd seen and loved several of the iconic films he has written and acted in and I knew that he'd come out early on Snowden's side with "The Snowden Principle," an essay he wrote only days after the story broke and the US government was calling for Snowden's head.[1] We had had conversations that usually lasted several hours, but I embraced Cusack as a true comrade only after I opened his freezer and found nothing but an old brass bus horn and a pair of small antlers.

I told him that I would love to meet Edward Snowden in Moscow.

The other person who would be travelling with us was Daniel Ellsberg—the Snowden of the '60s—the whistleblower who made public the Pentagon Papers during the war in Vietnam. I had met Dan briefly, more than ten years ago, when he gave me his book, *Secrets: A Memoir of Vietnam and the Pentagon Papers.*[2]

Dan comes down pretty ruthlessly on himself in his book. Only by reading it—and you should—can you even begin to understand the disquieting combination of guilt and pride he has lived with for about fifty of his eighty-four years. This makes Dan a complicated, conflicted man—half-hero, half-haunted specter—a man who has tried to do penance for his past deeds by speaking, writing, protesting, and getting arrested in acts of civil disobedience for decades.

In the first few chapters of *Secrets*, he tells of how, in 1965, when he was a young employee at the Pentagon, orders came straight from Robert McNamara's office (it "was like an order from God") to gather "'atrocity' details" about Viet Cong attacks on civilians and military bases anywhere in Vietnam.[3] McNamara, secretary of defense at the time, needed the information to justify "retaliatory" action—which essentially meant he needed a justification for bombing South Vietnam.[4] The "atrocity" gatherer that "God" chose was Daniel Ellsberg:

> I had no doubts or hesitation as I went down to the Joint War Room to do my best. That's the memory I have to deal with. . . . Briefly I told the colonel I needed details of atrocities. . . . Above all, I wanted gory details of the injuries to the Americans at Pleiku and especially at Qui Nhon. I told the colonel, "I need blood." . . . Most of the reports didn't go into such details, but some of them did. The district chief had been disembhow-eled in front of the whole village, and his family, his wife and four children, had been killed too. "Great! That's what I want to know! That's what we need! More of that. Can you find other stories like that?"[5]

Within weeks, the campaign called Rolling Thunder was announced. American jets began to bomb South Vietnam. Something like a hundred and seventy-five thousand marines were deployed in that small country on the other side of the world, eight thousand miles away from Washington, DC. The war would go on for eight more years. (According to the testimonies in the recently published book about the US war in Vietnam, *Kill Anything That Moves* by Nick Turse, what the US Army did in Vietnam as it moved from village to village with orders to "kill anything that moves"—which included women, children, and livestock—was just as vicious, though on a much larger scale, as anything ISIS is doing now. It had the added benefit of being backed up by the most powerful air force in the world.[6])

By the end of the war, three million Vietnamese people and fifty-eight thousand US troops had been killed and enough bombs had been dropped to cover the whole of Vietnam in several inches of steel.[7] Here's Dan again: "I have never been able to explain to myself—so I can't explain to anyone else—why I stayed in my Pentagon

job after the bombing started. Simple careerism isn't an adequate explanation; I wasn't wedded to that role or to more research from the inside; I'd learned as much as I needed to. That night's work was the worst thing I've ever done."[8]

When I first read *Secrets*, I was unsettled by my admiration and sympathy for Dan on the one hand and my anger, not at him of course, but at what he so candidly admitted to having been part of on the other. Those two feelings ran on clear, parallel tracks, refusing to converge. I knew that when my raw nerves met his, we would be friends, which is how it turned out.

Perhaps my initial unease, my inability to react simply and generously to what was clearly an act of courage and conscience on Dan's part, had to do with my having grown up in Kerala, where, in 1957, one of the first-ever democratically elected Communist governments in the world came to power. So, like Vietnam, we too had jungles, rivers, rice fields, and Communists. I grew up in a sea of red flags, workers' processions, and chants of *"Inquilab Zindabad!"* ("Long Live the Revolution!") Had a strong wind blown the Vietnam War a couple of thousand miles westward, I would have been a "gook"—a kill-able, bomb-able, Napalm-able type—another body to add local color in *Apocalypse Now*. (Hollywood won the Vietnam War, even if America didn't. And Vietnam is a Free Market Economy now. So who am I to be taking things to heart all these years later?)

But back then, in Kerala, we didn't need the Pentagon Papers to make us furious about the Vietnam War. I remember as a very young child speaking at my first school debate, dressed as a Viet Cong woman, in my mother's printed sarong. I spoke with tutored indignation about the "Running Dogs of Imperialism." I played with children called Lenin and Stalin. (There weren't any little Leons or baby Trotskys around—maybe they'd have been exiled or shot.) Instead of the Pentagon Papers, we could have done with some whistle-blowing about the reality of Stalin's purges or China's Great Leap Forward and the millions who perished in them.[9] But all that was dismissed by the Communist parties as Western propaganda or explained away as a necessary part of Revolution.

Despite my reservations and criticism of the various Communist parties in India (my novel *The God of Small Things* was denounced by the Communist Party of India (Marxist) in Kerala as anti-Communist), I believe that the decimation of the Left (by which I do not mean the defeat of the Soviet Union or the fall of the Berlin Wall) has led us to the embarrassingly foolish place we find ourselves in right now. Even capitalists must surely admit that, intellectually at least, socialism is a worthy opponent. It imparts intelligence even to its adversaries. Our tragedy today is not just that millions of people who called themselves communist or socialist were physically liquidated in Vietnam, Indonesia, Iran, Iraq, Afghanistan, not just that China and Russia, after all that revolution, have become capitalist economies, not just that the working class has been ruined in the United States and its unions dismantled, not just that Greece has been brought to its knees, or that Cuba will soon be assimilated into the free market—it is also that the language of the Left, the *discourse* of the Left, has been marginalized and is sought to be eradicated. The debate—even though the protagonists on both sides betrayed everything they claimed to believe in—used to be about social justice, equality, liberty, and redistribution of wealth. All we seem to be left with now is paranoid gibberish about a War on Terror whose whole purpose is to expand the War, increase the Terror, and obfuscate the fact that the wars of today are not aberrations but systemic, logical exercises to preserve a way of life whose delicate pleasures and exquisite comforts can only be delivered to the chosen few by a continuous, protracted war for hegemony—Lifestyle Wars.

What I wanted to ask Ellsberg and Snowden was, can these be *kind* wars? *Considerate* wars? *Good* wars? Wars that respect human rights?

The comical understudy for what used to be a conversation about justice is what the *New York Times* recently called "Bill and Melinda Gates's Pillow Talk" about "what they have learned from giving away $34 billion," which, according to a back-of-the-envelope calculation by the *Times* columnist Nicholas Kristof, has saved the lives of thirty-three million children from diseases like polio:

> "On the [Gates] foundation, there's always a lot
> of pillow talk," Melinda said. "We do push hard
> on each other." . . . Bill thought Melinda focused
> too much on field visits, while Melinda thought
> Bill spent too much time with officials. . . . They
> also teach each other, Melinda says. In the case of
> gender, they've followed her lead in investing in
> contraception but also they developed new metrics to satisfy Bill. So among their lessons learned
> from 15 years of philanthropy, one applies to any
> couple . . . *Listen to your spouse!*[10]

They plan—the article says without irony—to save sixty-one million more children's lives in the next fifteen years. (That, going by the same back-of-the-envelope calculation, would cost another $61 billion, at least.) All that money in one boardroom-bed—how do they sleep at night, Bill and Melinda? If you are nice to them and draw up a good project proposal, they may give you a grant so that you can also save the world in your own small way.

But seriously—what is one couple doing with that much money, which is just a small percentage of the indecent profits they make from Microsoft? And even that small percentage runs into billions. It's enough to set the world's agenda, enough to buy government policy, determine university curricula, fund NGOs and activists. It gives them the power to bend the whole world to their will. Forget the politics, is that even polite? Even if it's "good" will? Who's to decide what's good and what's not?

So that, roughly, is where we are right now, politically speaking.

Coming back to the 3 a.m. phone call—by dawn I was worrying about my air ticket and getting a Russian visa. I learned that I needed a hard copy of a confirmed hotel booking in Moscow, sealed and approved by the Ministry of Something or Other in Russia. How the hell was I to do that? I had only three days. John's wizard assistant organized it and couriered it to me. My heart missed a beat when I saw it. The Ritz-Carlton. My last political outing had been some weeks spent walking with Maoist guerrillas and sleeping underneath the stars in the Dandakaranya forest. And this next one was going to be in the *Ritz*? It wasn't just the money, it was ... I don't know ... I had never imagined the Ritz-Carlton as a base camp—or a venue—for any kind of real politics. (In any case, the Ritz has turned out to be the venue of choice for several Snowden interviews, including John Oliver's infamous conversation with him about "dick pics."[11])

I drove past the long, snaking queues outside the heavily guarded US consulate to get to the Russian embassy ... It was empty. There was nobody at the counters marked "passport," "visa forms," or "collection." There was no bell, no way of attracting anybody's attention. Through a half-open door, I caught an occasional, fleeting glimpse of people moving around in the backroom. No queue whatsoever in the embassy of a country with a history of every imaginable type of queue. Varlam Shalamov describes them so vividly in *Kolyma Tales*, his stories about the labor camp in Kolyma—queues for food, for shoes, for a meager scrap of clothing—a fight to the death over a piece of stale bread.[12] I remembered a poem about queues by Anna Akhmatova—who unlike many of her peers, had survived the Gulag. Well, sort of:

> *In the terrible years of the Yezhov terror, I spent*
> *seventeen months in the prison lines of Leningrad.*
> *Once, someone "recognized" me. Then a woman with*
> *bluish lips standing behind me, who, of course, had*

never heard me called by name before, woke up from
the stupor to which everybody had succumbed and
whispered in my ear (everyone spoke in whispers
   there):
"Can you describe this?"
And I answered: "Yes, I can."
Then something that looked like a smile passed over
what had once been her face.[13]

Akhmatova, her first husband Nikolay Gumilyov, Osip Mandelstam, and three other poets were part of Acmeism, a poets' guild. In 1921, Gumilyov was shot by a firing squad for counterrevolutionary activity. Mandelstam was arrested in 1934 for writing an ode to Stalin that showed signs of satire and was not convincing enough in its praise.[14] He died years later, starved and deranged, in a transit camp in Siberia. His poetry (which survived on scraps of paper hidden in pillow cases and cooking vessels, or committed to memory by people who loved him) was retrieved by his widow and by Anna Akhmatova.

This is the history of surveillance in the country that has offered asylum to Ed Snowden—wanted by the US government for exposing a surveillance apparatus that makes the operatives of the KGB and the Stasi look like preschool children. If the Snowden story were fiction, a good editor would dismiss its mirrored narrative symmetry as a cheap gimmick.

A man finally appeared at one of the counters at the Russian embassy and accepted my passport and visa form (as well as the sealed, stamped hard copy of the confirmation of my hotel booking). He asked me to come back the next morning.

When I got home, I went straight to my bookshelf, looking for a passage I had marked long ago in Arthur Koestler's *Darkness at Noon*.[15] Comrade N. S. Rubashov, once a high-level officer in the Soviet government, has been arrested for treason. He reminisces in his prison cell:

> All our principles were right, but our results were wrong. This is a diseased century. We diagnosed the disease and its causes with microscopic exactness, but wherever we applied the healing knife a new sore appeared. Our will was hard and pure, we should have been loved by the people. But they hate us. Why are we so odious and detested?

> We brought you truth, and in our mouth it sounded a lie. We brought you freedom, and it looks in our hands like a whip. We brought you the living life, and where our voice is heard the trees wither and there is a rustling of dry leaves. We brought you the promise of the future, but our tongue stammered and barked . . .[16]

Read now, it sounds like pillow talk between two old enemies who have fought a long, hard war and can no longer tell each other apart.

John Cusack

Things That
Can and Cannot
Be Said
(Continued)

Over the next week or so, the logistics had to be planned. It was short notice and a bit of a mad scramble. Roy made her own arrangements, but I had in mind Dan Ellsberg's history as a nuclear weapons planner for America's retaliation to a possible Soviet first strike. In other words, he had only spent a few years of his life planning the physical obliteration of the Soviet Union. Nuclear secrets, domino theory—*he was in those rooms.* Then there were the 85-plus arrests for civil disobedience, one of those in Russia on the *Sirius*, the Greenpeace boat protesting Soviet nuclear testing.[1] But Dan's visa came. And mine came, too.

Meanwhile in India, some of Roy's worst fears had materialized. Eight months before, Narendra Modi had become the new prime minister of India. (In May, I received this text: *Election results are out. The fascists in a landslide. The phantoms are real. What you see is what you get.*)

I met up with Roy in London. She had been there for two weeks giving talks in Cambridge and the Southbank Centre on her new work on Gandhi and B. R. Ambedkar.[2] At Heathrow, she told me quite casually that some folks in India were burning effigies of her. "I seem to be goading the Gandhians to violence," she laughed, "but I was disappointed with the quality of the effigy."

We flew together to Stockholm to meet up with Dan, who was attending the ceremony of the Right Livelihood Awards—some call it the Alternative Nobel—because Ed was one of the laureates.[3] We would fly to Moscow together from there.

The Stockholm streets were so clean you could eat off the ground.

On our first night, there was a dinner at a nautical museum with the complete salvaged wreckage of a huge 17th-century wooden warship as the centerpiece of the modernist structure. The *Vasa*, considered the

Titanic of Swedish disasters, was built on the orders of
yet another power-hungry king who wanted control of
seas and the future. It was so overloaded with weapons
and top-heavy, it capsized and sank before it even left
the harbor.

It was a classic human rights evening, to be sure: gour-
met food and good intentions, a choir singing beautiful
noels. I enjoyed watching the almost pathologically
anti-gala Roy trying to mask her blind panic. Not her

venue, as they say. Dan was busy and in great demand, meeting people, doing interviews. We caught occasional glimpses of him—and managed to say a quick hello.

The awards ceremony took place in the Swedish Parliament. Roy and I were graciously invited. We were late. It occurred to us that if neither of us would be comfortable sitting in the parliament halls of our own countries, what the fuck would we be doing sitting in the Swedish Parliament? So we skulked around the corridors like petty criminals until we found a cramped balcony from which we could watch the ceremony. Our empty seats reflected back at us. The speeches were long. We slipped away and walked through the great chambers and found an empty banquet hall with a laid out feast. There was a metaphor there somewhere. I switched on my recorder again.

JC: What is the meaning of charity as a political tool?

AR: It's an old joke, right? If you want to control somebody, support them. Or marry them.

(*Laughter*)

JC: Sugar daddy politics . . .

AR: Embrace the resistance, seize it, fund it.

JC: Domesticate it . . .

AR: Make it depend on you. Turn it into an art project or a product of some kind. The minute what you think of as radical becomes an institutionalized, funded operation, you're in some trouble. And it's cleverly done. It's not all bad . . . some are doing genuinely good work.

JC: Like the ACLU (American Civil Liberties Union) . . .

AR: They have money from the Ford Foundation, right? But they do excellent work. You can't fault people for the work they're doing, taken individually.

JC: People want to do something good, something useful . . .

AR: Yes. And it is these good intentions that are dragooned and put to work. It's a complicated thing. Think of a bead necklace. The beads on their own may be lovely, but when they're threaded together, they're not really free to skitter around as they please. When you look around and see how many NGOs are on, say, the Gates, Rockefeller, or Ford Foundation's handout list, there has to be something wrong, right? They turn potential radicals into receivers of their largesse—and then, very subtly, without appearing to—they circumscribe the boundaries of radical politics. And you're sacked if you disobey . . . sacked, unfunded, whatever. And then there's always the game of pitting the "funded" against the "unfunded," in which the funder takes center stage. So, I mean, I'm not against people being funded—because we're running out of options—but we have to understand—are you walking the dog or is the dog walking you? Or who's the dog and who is you?

JC: I'm definitely the dog . . . and I've definitely been walked.

AR: Everywhere—not just in America . . . repress, beat up, shoot, jail those you can, and throw money at those whom you can't—and gradually sandpaper the edge off them. They're in the business of creating what we in India call *Paaltu Sher*, which means Tamed Tigers. Like a pretend resistance . . . so you can let off steam without damaging anything.

JC: The first time you spoke at the World Social Forum . . . when was that?

AR: In 2003, in Porto Alegre . . . just before the US invasion of Iraq.[4]

JC: And then you went the next year in Mumbai and it was . . .

AR: . . . totally NGO-ized.[5] So many major activists had turned into travel agents, just having to organize tickets and money, flying people up and down. The forum suddenly declared, "Only nonviolence, no armed struggles . . ." They had turned Gandhian.

JC: So anyone involved in armed resistance . . .

AR: All out, all out. Many of the radical struggles were out. And I thought, fuck this. My question is, if, let's say, there are people who live in villages deep in the forest, four days' walk from anywhere, and a thousand soldiers arrive and burn their villages and kill and rape people to scare them off their land because mining companies want it—what brand of nonviolence would the stalwarts of the establishment recommend? Nonviolence is radical political theater.

JC: Effective only when there's an audience . . .

AR: *Exactly.* And who can pull in an audience? You need some capital, some stars, right? Gandhi was a superstar. The indigenous people in the forest don't have that capital, that drawing power. So they have no audience. Nonviolence should be a tactic—not an ideology preached from the sidelines to victims of *massive* violence . . . With me, it's been an evolution of seeing through these things.

" Gandhi was a superstar. The indigenous people in the forest don't have that capital, that drawing power. So they have no audience. Nonviolence should be a tactic—not an ideology preached from the sidelines to victims of *massive* violence. "

JC: You begin to smell the digestive enzymes . . .

AR: (*Laughing*) But you know, the revolution cannot be funded. It's not the imagination of trusts and foundations that's going to bring real change.

JC: But what's the bigger game that we can name?

AR: The bigger game is keeping the world safe for the Free Market. Structural Adjustment, Privatization, Free Market fundamentalism—all masquerading as Democracy and the Rule of Law. Many corporate foundation–funded NGOs—not all, but many—become the missionaries of the "new economy." They tinker with your imagination, with language. The idea of "human rights," for example—sometimes it bothers me. Not in itself, but because the concept of human rights has replaced the much grander idea of justice. Human rights are fundamental rights, they are the minimum, the very least we demand. Too often, they become the goal itself. What should be the *minimum* becomes the *maximum*— all we are supposed to expect—but human rights aren't enough. The goal is, and must always be, justice.

JC: The term *human rights* is, or can be, a kind of pacifier—filling the space in the political imagination that justice deserves?

AR: Look at the Israel-Palestine conflict, for example. If you look at a map from 1947 to now, you'll see that Israel has gobbled up almost all of Palestinian land with its illegal settlements. To talk about justice in that battle, you have to talk about those settlements. But, if you just talk about human rights, then you can say, "Oh, Hamas violates human rights," "Israel violates human rights." Ergo, both are bad.

Landownership in Palestine and the UN Partition Plan, 1947

Palestinian Villages Depopulated in 1948 and 1967, and Razed by Israel

Palestinian Academic Society for the Study of International Affairs (PASSIA)

JC: You can turn it into an equivalence . . .

AR: . . . though it isn't one. But this discourse of human rights, it's a very good format for TV—the great atrocity analysis and condemnation industry (*laughs*). Who comes out smelling sweet in the atrocity analysis? States have invested themselves with the right to legitimize violence—so who gets criminalized and delegitimized? Only—or well that's excessive—*usually*, the resistance.

JC: So the term *human rights* can take the oxygen out of justice?

AR: Human rights takes *history* out of justice.

JC: Justice always has context . . .

AR: I sound as though I'm trashing human rights . . . I'm not. All I'm saying is that the idea of justice—even just dreaming of justice—is revolutionary. The language of human rights tends to accept a status quo that is intrinsically unjust—and then tries to make it more accountable. But then, of course, the catch-22 is that violating human rights is *integral* to the project of neoliberalism and global hegemony.

JC: . . . As there's no other way of implementing those policies except violently.

AR: No way at all—but talk loud enough about human rights and it gives the impression of democracy at work, justice at work. There was a time when the United States waged war to topple democracies, because back then democracy was a threat to the Free Market. Countries were nationalizing their resources, protecting their markets. . . . So then, real democracies were being toppled. They were toppled in Iran, they were toppled all across Latin America, Chile . . .

JC: The list is too long . . .

AR: Now we're in a situation where democracy has been taken into the workshop and fixed, remodeled to be market friendly. So now the United States is fighting wars to install democracies. First it was topple them, now it's install them, right? And this whole rise of corporate-funded NGOs in the modern world, this notion of CSR, corporate social responsibility—it's all part of a New Managed Democracy. In that sense, it's all part of the same machine.

JC: Tentacles of the same squid.

AR: They moved in to the spaces that were left when "structural adjustment" forced states to pull back on public spending—on health, education, infrastructure, water supply—turning what ought to be people's rights, to education, to health care, and so on, into charitable activity available to a few. Peace, Inc. is sometimes as worrying as War, Inc. It's a way of managing public anger. We're all being managed, and we don't even know it. . . . The IMF and the World Bank, the most opaque and secretive entities, put millions into NGOs who fight against "corruption" and for "transparency." They want the Rule of Law—as long as they make the laws. They want transparency in order to standardize a situation, so that global capital can flow without any impediment. Cage the People, Free the Money. The only thing that is allowed to move freely—unimpeded—around the world today is money . . . capital.

JC: It's all for efficiency, right? Stable markets, stable world . . . there's a great violence in the idea of a uniform "investment climate."

AR: In India, that's a phrase we use interchangeably with "massacre." Stable markets, *unstable* world. Efficiency. Everybody hears about it. It's enough to make you want to be pro-inefficiency and pro-corruption. (*Laughing*) But seriously, if you look at the history of the Ford Foundation and Rockefeller, in Latin America, in Indonesia, where almost a million people, mainly Communists, were killed by General Suharto, who was backed by the CIA, in South Africa, in the US civil rights movement—or even now, it's very disturbing.[6] They have always worked closely with the US State Department.

JC: And yet now Ford funds *The Act of Killing*—the film about those same massacres.[7] They profile the butchers ... but not their masters. They won't follow the money.

AR: They have so much money, they can fund everything, very bad things as well as very good things— documentary films, nuclear weapons planners, gender rights, feminist conferences, literature and film festivals, university chairs ... anything, as long as it doesn't upset the "market" and the economic status quo. One of Ford's "good works" was to fund the CFR, the Council on Foreign Relations, which worked closely with the CIA.[8] The first eleven World Bank presidents were from the CFR.[9] Ford funded RAND, the research and development corporation which works closely with the US defense forces.

JC: That was where Dan worked. That's where he laid his hands on the Pentagon Papers.

AR: The Pentagon Papers ... I couldn't believe what I was reading ... that stuff about bombing dams, planning famines.... I wrote an introduction to an edition of Noam Chomsky's *For Reasons of State* in which he analyzes the Pentagon Papers.[100] There was a chapter in the book called "The Backroom Boys"—maybe that wasn't the Pentagon Papers part, I don't remember . . . but there was a letter or a note of some kind, maybe from soldiers in the field, about how great it was that white phosphorus had been mixed in with napalm . . . "The original product wasn't so hot—if the gooks were quick they could scrape it off. So the boys started adding polystyrene—now it sticks like shit to a blanket. [T]hen . . . they started adding Willie Peter [WP—white phosphorus] so's to make it burn better."[11] Nice people no?

JC: You remember that by rote?

AR: I can't forget it. It burned me to the bone . . . I grew up in Kerala, remember. Communist country . . .

JC: You were talking about how the Ford Foundation funded RAND and the CFR.

AR: (*Laughs*) Yes . . . it's a bedroom comedy . . . actually a bedroom tragedy . . . is that a genre? Ford funded CFR and RAND. Robert McNamara moved from heading Ford Motors to the Pentagon. So, as you can see, we're encircled.

JC: . . . and not just by the past.

AR: No—by the future, too. The future is Google, isn't it? In Julian Assange's book—brilliant book—*When Google Met WikiLeaks*, he suggests that there isn't much daylight between Google and the NSA.[12] The three people who went along with Eric Schmidt—CEO of Google—to interview Julian were Jared Cohen, director of Google Ideas—ex-State Department and senior something or other on the CFR, adviser to Condoleezza Rice and Hillary Clinton. The two others were Lisa Shields and Scott Malcolmson, also former State Department and CFR. It's serious shit. But when we talk about NGOs, there's something we must be careful about . . .

JC: What's that?

AR: When the attack on NGOs comes from the opposite end, from the far Right, then those of us who've been criticizing NGOs from a completely different perspective will look terrible . . . to liberals, we'll be the bad guys . . .

JC: Once again pitting the "funded" against the "unfunded."

AR: For example, in India the new government—the members of the radical Hindu Right who want India to be a "Hindu Nation"—they're bigots. Butchers. Massacres are their unofficial election campaigns—orchestrated to polarize communities and bring in the vote. It was so in Gujarat in 2002, and this year, in the run-up to the general elections, in a place called Muzaffarnagar, after which tens of thousands of Muslims had to flee from their villages and live in camps.[13] Some of those who are accused of all that murdering are now cabinet ministers. Their support for straightforward, chest-thumping butchery makes you long for even the hypocrisy of the human rights discourse. But now if the "human rights" NGOs make a noise, or even whisper too loudly . . . this government will shut them down. And it can, very easily. All it has to do is to go after the funders . . . and the funders, whoever they are, especially those who are interested in India's huge "market," will either cave in or scuttle over to the other side. Those NGOs will blow over because they're a chimera, they don't have deep roots in society among the people, really, so they'll just disappear. Even the pretend resistance that has sucked the marrow out of genuine resistance will be gone.

JC: Is Modi going to succeed long term?

AR: It's hard to say. There's no real opposition, you know? He has an absolute majority and a government that he completely controls, and he himself—and I think this is true of most people with murky pasts—doesn't trust any of his own people, so he's become this person who has to interface directly with people. The government is secondary. Public institutions are being peopled by his acolytes, school and university syllabi are being revamped, history is being rewritten in absurd ways. It's very dangerous, all of it. And a large section of young people, students, the IT crowd, the educated middle class and, of course, Big Business, are with him—the Hindu right wing is with him. He's lowering the bar of public discourse—saying things like, "Oh, Hindus discovered plastic surgery in the Vedas because how else would we have had an elephant-headed god."[14]

JC: (*Laughing*) He said that?

AR: Yes! It's dangerous. On the other hand, it's so corny that I don't know how long it can last. But for now people are wearing Modi masks and waving back at him . . . He was democratically elected. There's no getting away from that. That's why when people say "the people" or "the public" as though it's the final repository of all morality, I sometimes flinch.

JC: As they say, "Kitsch is the mask of Death" . . . [15]

AR: Sounds about right . . . But then, while there's no real opposition to him in Parliament, India's a very interesting place . . . there's no formal opposition, but there's genuine on-the-ground opposition. If you travel around—there are all kinds of people, brilliant people . . . journalists, activists, filmmakers, whether you go to Kashmir, the Indian part, or to an Adivasi village about to be submerged by a dam reservoir—the level of understanding of everything we've talked about—surveillance, globalization, NGO-ization—is so high, you know? The wisdom of the resistance movements, which are ragged and tattered and pushed to the wall, is incredible. So . . . I look to them and keep the faith. (*Laughs*)

JC: So this isn't new to you . . . the debate about mass surveillance?

AR: Of course, the details are new to me, the technical stuff and the scale of it all—but for many of us in India who don't consider ourselves "innocent," surveillance is something we have all always been aware of. Most of those who have been summarily executed by the army or the police—we call them "encounters"—have been tracked down using their cellphones. In Kashmir, for years they have monitored every phone call, every e-mail, every Facebook account—that plus beating doors down, shooting into crowds, mass arrests, torture that puts Abu Ghraib in the shade. It's the same in central India.

JC: In the forest where you went "walking with the comrades"?

AR: Yes. Where the poorest people in the world have stopped some of the richest mining corporations in their tracks. The great irony is that people who live in remote areas, who are illiterate and don't own TVs, are in some ways more free because they are beyond the reach of indoctrination by the modern mass media. There's a virtual civil war going on there and few know about it. Anyway, before I went into the forest, I was told by the superintendent of police, "Out there, ma'am . . . my boys shoot to kill."[16] The police call the area across the river "Pakistan."[17] Anyway, then the cop says to me, "'See, ma'am, frankly speaking this problem can't be solved by us police or military. The problem with these tribals is they don't understand greed. Unless they become greedy there's no hope for us. I have told my boss, remove the force and instead put a TV in every home. Everything will be automatically sorted out."[18] His point was that watching TV would teach them greed.

JC: Greed. . . . That's what this whole circus is about, huh?

AR: Yes.

That evening, after the awards ceremony, we met up with Dan. The next morning, we caught the flight to Moscow. Traveling with us was Ole von Uexküll from the Right Livelihood Foundation, a lovely man with clear eyes and impeccable manners. Ole was going to give Ed the prize since he couldn't travel to Stockholm to receive it. Ole would be our companion for the next few days. On the flight, Dan was furiously reading Roy's new essay, "The Doctor and the Saint," scribbling notes on a yellow legal pad.[19] My mind began to race, wondering what Roy was making of this mini flying circus hurtling toward Moscow. What I would learn from what she calls—with sinister silkiness and mischief twinkling in her dark brown eyes—"the gook perspective"? She can disarm you at any time with her friendly hustler's grin,

but her eyes see things and love things so fiercely, it's frightening at times.

Going through immigration of the country he once planned to annihilate, Dan flashed the peace sign. Soon we were driving through the freezing streets of Moscow. The Ritz-Carlton is perched literally a few hundred yards from the Kremlin. The Red Square always seemed so much bigger on TV, during all those horror show military parades. It's so much smaller to the naked eye. We checked in and were whisked up to a VIP reception lounge with great views of the Kremlin and an Audi car display on its roof deck: *The Ritz Terrace Brought to You by Audi.* Another reminder hanging over Lenin's tomb that capitalism had supposedly ended history.

At noon the next day, I got the call I was waiting for in my room.

The meeting between these two living symbols of American conscience was historic. It needed to happen. Seeing Ed and Dan together, trading stories, exchanging notes, was both heartwarming and deeply inspiring, and the conversation with Roy and the two former President's Men was extraordinary. It had depth, insight, wit, generosity, and a lightness of touch not possible in a formal, structured interview. Aware that we were being watched and monitored by forces greater than ourselves, we talked. Maybe one day the NSA will give us the minutes of our meeting. What was remarkable was how much agreement there was in the room. It wasn't just what was said, but the way it was said, not just the text, but the subtext, warmth, and laughter that was so exhilarating. But that's another story. After two unforgettable days and twenty hours spent together, we said goodbye to Ed, wondering if we'd ever see him again.

During the last few hours with Ed, Dan had recounted in horrifying and empirical detail the history of the

nuclear arms race—a history of lies—an apocalyptic tome of charnel monologues and murder rites.

At one point, Dan referred to Robert McNamara, his boss in the Pentagon, as a "moderate." Roy's eyes snapped wide open at the assertion. Dan then explained how, compared to the other lunatics in the Pentagon like Edward Teller and Curtis LeMay, he was one. McNamara's moderate and reasonable argument, Dan said, was that the United States needed only four hundred warheads instead of a thousand. Because after four hundred, there were "diminishing returns on genocide." It begins to flatten out. "You kill most people with four hundred, so if you have eight hundred, you don't kill that many more—four hundred warheads would kill 1.2 billion people out of the then total population of 3.7 billion. So why have a thousand?"

Roy listened to all this without saying very much. In "The End of Imagination," the essay she wrote after India's 1998 nuclear tests, she had gotten herself into serious trouble when she declared, "If protesting against having a nuclear bomb implanted in my brain is anti-Hindu and antinational, then I secede. I hereby declare myself an independent, mobile republic."[20] Dan, who is writing a book on the nuclear arms race, told me it was one of the finest things he's ever read on the subject. "Wouldn't you say," Roy said for the record, or to anybody willing to listen, "that nuclear weapons are the inevitable, toxic corollary of the idea of the Great Nation?"

Just after Ed left, Dan collapsed on to my bed—exhausted and blissful—with his arms stretched wide, but then a deep storm erupted. He became distressed and emotional. He quoted from "The Man Without a Country" by Edward Everett Hale, a short story about an American naval officer who was tried and court martialed.[21] Hale's sentence was that he should forever go from ship to ship, and he should never hear the name "America" again. In the story, a character quotes the poem "Patriotism" by Sir Walter Scott:

> Breathes there the man, with soul so dead,
> Who never to himself hath said,
> "This is my own, my native land!"[22]

Dan began to weep. Through his tears, he said, "I'm still that much of a patriot in some sense . . . not for the State, but. . . ." He talked about his son and how he came of age during the war in Vietnam, and how he, Dan, used to think his son was born for jail. "That the best thing that the best people in our country like Ed can do is to go to prison . . . or be an exile in Russia? This is what it's come to in my country . . . it's horrible, you know. . . ." Roy's eyes were sympathetic but distinctly unsettled.

It was our last night in Moscow. We went for a walk in the Red Square. The Kremlin was lit with fairy lights. Dan went off to buy himself a Cossack fur hat. We stepped carefully on to the treacherous sheet of ice that covered the Red Square, trying to guess where Putin's window might be and whether he was still at work. Roy kept talking as if she were still in Room 1001.

AR: The diminishing returns of genocide . . . what's the subject heading? Math or economics? Zoology it should be. Mao said he was prepared to have millions of Chinese people perish in a nuclear war as long as China survived. . . . I'm beginning to find it more and more sick that only humans make it into our calculations. . . . Annihilate life on earth, but save the nation . . . what's the subject heading? Stupidity or Insanity?

JC: Social Service . . . What do you think those maniacs look like in binary code?

AR: Good-looking. When you think of how much violence, how much blood . . . how much has been destroyed to create the great nations, America, Australia, Britain, Germany, France, Belgium—even India, Pakistan.

JC: The Soviet Union . . .

AR: Yes. Having destroyed so much to make them, we must have nuclear weapons to protect them—and climate change to hold up their way of life . . . a two-pronged annihilation project.

JC: We must all bow down to the flags.

AR: And—I might as well say it now that I'm in the Red Square—to capitalism. Every time I say the word *capitalism*, everyone just assumes . . .

JC: You must be a Marxist.

AR: I have plenty of Marxism in me, I do . . . but Russia and China had their bloody revolutions and even while they were Communist, they had the same idea about generating wealth—tear it out of the bowels of the earth. And now they have come out with the same idea in the end . . . you know, capitalism. But capitalism will fail, too. We need a new imagination. Until then, we're all just out here . . .

JC: Wandering . . .

AR: Thousands of years of ideological, philosophical, and practical decisions were made. They altered the surface of the earth, the coordinates of our souls. For every one of those decisions, maybe there's another decision that could have been made, should have been made.

JC: *Can* be made . . .

AR: Of course. So I don't have the Big Idea. I don't have the arrogance to even want to have the Big Idea. But I believe the physics of resisting power is as old as the physics of accumulating power. That's what keeps the balance in the universe . . . the refusal to obey. I mean what's a country? It's just an administrative unit, a glorified municipality. Why do we imbue it with esoteric meaning and protect it with nuclear bombs? I can't bow down to a municipality . . . it's just not intelligent. The bastards will do what they have to do, and we'll do what we have to do. Even if they annihilate us, we'll go down on the other side.

I looked at Roy, and wondered what trouble awaited her back in India[23] . . . an old Yugoslavian proverb came to mind—"Tell the truth and run." But some creatures will not run . . . even when maybe they should. They know that to show weakness only emboldens the bastards . . .

Suddenly she turned to me and thanked me formally for organizing the meeting with Edward Snowden. "He presents himself as this cool systems man, but it's only passion that could make him do what he did. He's not just a systems man. That's what I needed to know."

We kept an eye on Dan in the distance bargaining with the hat-seller. I was worried he might slip on the ice.

"So, for the record, Ms. Roy," I asked, "as someone with 'plenty of Marxism' in her, how does it feel to be walking on ice in the Red Square?" She nodded sagely, appearing to give my talk-show question serious consideration. "I think it should be privatized . . . handed over to a foundation that works tirelessly for the empowerment of women prisoners, abolishing of child labor, and the improvement of relations between mass media and mining companies. Maybe to Bill and Melinda Gates."

She grinned with sadness in it . . . I could almost hear the chimes of harmonic thinking, as clear as the church bells that suddenly filled the frozen air and the wind that chopped through the bleak winter night.

"Listen, man," she said. "God's back in the Red Square."

Arundhati Roy

What Shall
We Love?

The Moscow Un-Summit wasn't a formal interview. Nor was it a cloak-and-dagger underground rendezvous. The upshot is that we didn't get the cautious, diplomatic, regulation Edward Snowden. The downshot (that isn't a word, I know) is that the jokes, the humor, and repartee that took place in Room 1001 cannot be reproduced. The Un-Summit cannot be written about in the detail that it deserves. Yet it definitely cannot *not* be written about. Because it did happen. And because the world is a millipede that inches forward on millions of real conversations. And this, certainly, was a real one.

What mattered, perhaps even more than what was said, was the spirit in the room. There was Edward Snowden who after 9/11 was in his own words "straight up singing highly of Bush" and signing up for the war in Iraq. And there were those of us who after 9/11 had been straight up doing exactly the opposite. It was a little late for this conversation, of course. Iraq has been all but destroyed. And now the map of what is so condescendingly called the "Middle East" is being brutally redrawn (yet again). But still, there we were, all of us, talking to each other in a bizarre hotel in Russia.

Bizarre it certainly was. The opulent lobby of the Moscow Ritz-Carlton was teeming with drunk million-aires, high on new money, and gorgeous, high-stepping young women, half-peasant, half-supermodel, draped on the arms of toady men—gazelles on their way to fame and fortune, paying their dues to the satyrs who would get them there. In the corridors, you passed seri-ous fistfights, loud singing, and quiet, liveried waiters wheeling trolleys with towers of food and silverware in and out of rooms. In Room 1001 we were so close to the Kremlin that if you put your hand out of the window, you could almost touch it. It was snowing outside. We were deep into the Russian winter—never credited enough for its part in the Second World War.

Edward Snowden was much smaller than I thought

he'd be. Small, lithe, neat, like a housecat. He greeted
Dan ecstatically and us warmly.

"I know why you're here," he said to me smiling.

"Why?"

"To radicalize me."

I laughed. We settled down on various perches, stools,
chairs, and John's bed.

Dan and Ed were so pleased to meet each other, and
had so much to say to each other, that it felt a little
impolite to intrude on them. At times they broke into
some kind of arcane code language: "I jumped from
nobody on the street straight to TSSCI." "No, because,
again, this isn't DS at all, this is NSA. At CIA, it's called
COMO." ". . . It's kind of a similar role, but is it under
support?" "PRISEC or PRIVAC?" "They start out with
the TALENT-KEYHOLE thing. Everyone then gets read
into TS, SI, TK, and GAMMA—G clearance . . . Nobody
knows what it is . . ."[1]

It took a while before I felt it was alright to interrupt
them. Snowden's disarming answer to my question about
being photographed cradling the American flag was to
roll his eyes and say: "Oh, man. I don't know. Somebody

handed me a flag, they took a picture." And when I asked him why he signed up for the war in Iraq, when millions of people all over the world were marching against it, he replied, equally disarmingly: "I fell for the propaganda."

Dan talked at some length about how it would be unusual for US citizens who joined the Pentagon and the NSA to have read much literature on US exceptionalism and its history of warfare. (And once they joined, it was unlikely to be a subject that interested them.) He and Ed had watched it play out live, in real time, and were horrified enough to stake their lives and their freedom when they decided to be whistleblowers. What the two of them clearly had in common was a strong, almost corporeal sense of moral righteousness—of right and wrong. A sense of righteousness that was obviously at work not just when they decided to blow the whistle on what they thought to be morally unacceptable, but also when they signed up for their jobs—Dan to save his country from Communism, Ed to save it from Islamist terrorism. What they did when they grew disillusioned was so electrifying, so dramatic, that they have come to be identified by that single act of moral courage.

I asked Ed Snowden what he thought about Washington's ability to destroy countries and its inability to win a war (despite mass surveillance). I think the question was phrased quite rudely—something like "When was the last time the United States won a war?" We spoke about whether the economic sanctions and subsequent invasion of Iraq could be accurately called genocide. We talked about how the CIA knew—and was preparing for the fact—that the world was heading to a place of not just *inter*-country war but of *intra*-country war in which mass surveillance would be necessary to control populations. And about how armies were being turned into police forces to administer countries they have invaded and occupied, while the police, even in places like India and Pakistan and Ferguson, Missouri, in the United States, were being trained to behave like armies to quell internal insurrections.

Ed spoke at some length about "sleepwalking into a total surveillance state." And here I quote him, because he's said this often before:

> If we do nothing, we sort of sleepwalk into a total surveillance state where we have both a super-state that has unlimited capacity to apply force with an unlimited ability to know [about the people it is targeting]—and that's a very dangerous combination. That's the dark future. The fact that they know everything about us and we know nothing about them—because they are secret, they are privileged, and they are a separate class . . . the elite class, the political class, the resource class—we

don't know where they live, we don't know what they do, we don't know who their friends are. They have the ability to know all that about us. This is the direction of the future, but I think there are changing possibilities in this . . .

I asked Ed whether the NSA was just feigning annoyance at his revelations but might actually be secretly pleased at being known as the All Seeing, All Knowing Agency—because that would help to keep people fearful, off balance, always looking over their shoulders, and easy to manage.

Dan spoke about how even in the United States, a police state was only another 9/11 away: "We are not in a police state now, not yet. I'm talking about what may come. I realize I shouldn't put it that way . . . White, middle-class, educated people like myself are not living in a police state . . . Black, poor people are living in a police state. The repression starts with the semi-white, the Middle Easterners, including anybody who is allied with them, and goes on from there . . . We don't have a police state. One more 9/11, and then I believe we will have hundreds of thousands of detentions. Middle Easterners and Muslims will be put in detention camps or deported. After 9/11, we had thousands of people arrested without charges . . . But I'm talking about the future. I'm talking the level of the Japanese in World War II . . . I'm talking of hundreds of thousands in camps or deported. I think the surveillance is very relevant to that. They will know who to put away—the data is already collected." (When he said this, I did wonder, though I did not ask—how different would things have been if Snowden had not been white?)

We talked about war and greed, about terrorism, and what an accurate definition of it would be. We spoke about countries, flags, and the meaning of patriotism. We talked about public opinion and the concept of public morality and how fickle it could be, and how easily manipulated.

It wasn't a Q&A type of conversation. We were an incongruous gathering. Ole, myself, and three troublesome Americans. John Cusack, who thought up and organized this whole disruptive enterprise, comes from a fine tradition, too—of musicians, writers, actors, athletes who have refused to buy the bullshit, however beautifully it was packaged.

What will become of Edward Snowden? Will he ever be able to return to the United States? His chances don't look good. The US government—the Deep State, as well as both the major political parties—wants to punish him for the enormous damage he has inflicted, in their perception, on the security establishment. (It's got Chelsea

Manning and the other whistleblowers where it wants them.) If it does not manage to kill or jail Snowden, it must use everything in its power to limit the damage that he's done and continues to do. One of those ways is to try to contain, co-opt, and usher the debate around whistleblowing in a direction that suits it. And it has, to some extent, managed to do that. In the Public Security versus Mass Surveillance debate that is taking place in the establishment Western media, the Object of Love is America. America and her actions. Are they moral or immoral? Are they right or wrong? Are the whistleblowers American patriots or American traitors? Within this constricted matrix of morality, other countries, other cultures, other conversations—even if they are the victims of US wars—usually appear only as witnesses in the main trial. They either bolster the outrage of the prosecution or the indignation of the defense. The trial, when it is conducted on these terms, serves to reinforce the idea that there can be a moderate, moral superpower. Are we not witnessing it in action? Its heartache? Its guilt? Its self-correcting mechanisms? Its watchdog media? Its activists who will not stand for ordinary (innocent) American citizens being spied on by their own government? In these debates that appear to be fierce and intelligent, words like *public* and *security* and *terrorism* are thrown around, but they remain, as always, loosely defined and are used more often than not in the way the US state would like them to be used.

Is it shocking that Barack Obama approved a "kill list"?[2]

What sort of list do the millions of people who have been killed in all the US wars belong on, if not a "kill list"?

In all of this, Snowden, in exile, has to remain strategic and tactical. He's in the impossible position of having to negotiate the terms of his amnesty/trial with the very institutions in the United States that feel betrayed by him, and the terms of his domicile in Russia with that Great Humanitarian, Vladimir Putin. So the superpowers have the Truth-teller in a position where he now has to be extremely careful about how he uses the spotlight he has earned and what he says publicly.

Even still, leaving aside what cannot be said, the conversation around whistleblowing is a thrilling one—it's realpolitik—busy, important, and full of legalese. It has spies and spy-hunters, escapades, secrets, and secret-leakers. It's a very adult and absorbing universe of its own. However, if it becomes, as it sometimes threatens to, a substitute for broader, more radical political thinking, then the conversation that Daniel Berrigan, Jesuit priest, poet, and war resister (contemporary of Daniel Ellsberg), wanted to have when he said, "Every nation-state tends towards the imperial—that is the point," becomes a little inconvenient.

I was glad to see that when Snowden made his debut on Twitter (and chalked up half a million followers in half a second) he said, "I used to work for the government. Now I work for the public."[3] Implicit in that sentence is the belief that the government does not work for the public. That's the beginning of a subversive and inconvenient conversation. By "the government," of course, he means the US government, his former employer. But who does he mean by "the public"? The US public? Which part of the US public? He'll have to decide as he goes along. In democracies, the line between an elected government and "the public" is never all that clear. The elite is usually fused with the government pretty seamlessly. Viewed from an international perspective, if there really is such a thing as "the US public," it's a very privileged public indeed. The only "public" I know is a maddeningly tricky labyrinth.

Oddly, when I think back on the meeting in the Moscow Ritz, the memory that flashes up first in my mind is an image of Daniel Ellsberg. Dan, after all those hours of

Edward Snowden ✔
@Snowden

I used to work for the government. Now I work for the public. Director at @FreedomofPress.

talking, lying back on John's bed, Christ-like, with his arms flung open, weeping for what the United States has turned into—a country whose "best people" must either go to prison or into exile. I was moved by his tears but troubled, too—because they were the tears of a man who has seen the machine up close. A man who was once on a first-name basis with the people who controlled it and who coldly contemplated the idea of annihilating life on earth. A man who risked everything to blow the whistle on them. Dan knows all the arguments, for as well as against. He often uses the word *imperialism* to describe US history and foreign policy. He knows now, forty years after he made the Pentagon Papers public, that even though particular individuals have gone, the machine keeps on turning.

Daniel Ellsberg's tears made me think about love, about loss, about dreams—and, most of all, about failure.

What sort of love is this love that we have for countries? What sort of country is it that will ever live up to our dreams? What sort of dreams were these that have been broken? Isn't the greatness of great nations directly proportionate to their ability to be ruthless, genocidal? Doesn't the height of a country's "success" usually also mark the depths of its moral failure?

And what about *our* failure? Writers, artists, radicals, anti-nationals, mavericks, malcontents—what of the failure of our imaginations? What of our failure to replace the idea of flags and countries with a less lethal Object of Love? Human beings seem unable to live without war, but they are also unable to live without love. So the question is, what shall we love?

Writing this at a time when refugees are flooding into Europe—the result of decades of US and European foreign policy in the "Middle East"—makes me wonder: Who is a refugee? Is Edward Snowden a refugee? Surely, he is. Because of what he did, he cannot return to the place he thinks of as his country (although he *can* continue to live where he is most comfortable—inside the Internet). The refugees fleeing from wars in Afghanistan, Iraq, and Syria to Europe are refugees of the Lifestyle Wars. But the thousands of people in countries like India who are being jailed and killed by those same Lifestyle Wars, the millions who are being driven off their lands and farms, exiled from everything they have ever known—their language, their history, the landscape that formed them— are not. As long as their misery is contained within the arbitrarily drawn borders of their "own" country, they are not considered refugees. But they *are* refugees. And certainly, in terms of numbers, such people are the great majority in the world today. Unfortunately in imaginations that are locked down into a grid of countries and borders, in minds that are shrink-wrapped in flags, they don't make the cut.

Perhaps the best-known refugee of the Lifestyle Wars is Julian Assange, the founder and editor of WikiLeaks, who is currently serving his fourth year as a fugitive-guest in a room in the Ecuadorian embassy in London. The British police are stationed in a small lobby just outside the front door. There are snipers on the roof who have orders to arrest him, shoot him, drag him out if he so much as puts a toe out of the door, which for all legal purposes is an international border. The Ecuadorian embassy is located across the street from Harrods, the world's most famous department store. The day Dan, John, and I met Julian, Harrods was sucking in and spewing out frenzied Christmas shoppers in their hundreds, or perhaps even thousands. In the middle of that tony London high street, the smell of opulence and excess met the smell of incarceration and the Free World's fear of free speech. (They shook hands and agreed never to be friends.)

On the day (actually the night) we met Julian, we were not allowed by security to take phones, cameras, or any recording devices into the room. So that conversation also remains off the record.

Despite the odds stacked against its founder-editor,

WikiLeaks continues its work, as cool and insouciant as ever. Most recently it has offered $100,000 to anybody who can provide "smoking gun" documents about the Transatlantic Trade and Investment Partnership (TTIP), a free trade agreement between Europe and the United States that aims to give multinational corporations the power to sue sovereign governments that do things that adversely impact corporate profits.[4] Criminal acts could include governments increasing workers' minimum wages, not seen to be cracking down on "terrorist" villagers who impede the work of mining companies, or, say, having the temerity to turn down Monsanto's offer of genetically modified corporate-patented seeds. TTIP is just another weapon like intrusive surveillance or depleted uranium, to be used in the Lifestyle Wars.

Looking at Julian Assange sitting across the table from me, pale and worn, without having had five minutes of sunshine on his skin for nine hundred days, but still refusing to disappear or capitulate the way his enemies would like him to, I smiled at the idea that nobody thinks of him as an *Australian* hero or an *Australian* traitor. To his enemies, Assange has betrayed much more than a country. He has betrayed the ideology of the ruling powers. For this, they hate him even more than they hate Edward Snowden. And that's saying a lot.

We're told, often enough, that as a species we are poised on the edge of the abyss. It's possible that our puffed-up, prideful intelligence has outstripped our instinct for survival and the road back to safety has already been washed away. In which case there's nothing much to be done. If there is something to be done, then one thing is for sure: those who created the problem will not be the ones who come up with a solution. Encrypting our e-mails will help, but not very much. Recalibrating our understanding of what love means, what happiness means—and, yes, what countries mean—might. Recalibrating our priorities might. An old-growth forest, a mountain range, or a river valley is more important and certainly more lovable than any country will ever be. I could weep for a river valley, and I have. But for a country? Oh man, I don't know . . .

John Cusack,

Daniel Ellsberg,

Arundhati Roy,

and Edward Snowden

in Conversation

"Yes, Virginia, There Is a Missile Gap"

Peter Sellers · George C. Scott

in Stanley Kubrick's

Dr. Strangelove

Or:
How
I Learned
To
Stop
Worrying
And
Love
The
Bomb

the hot-line suspense comedy

also starring Sterling Hayden · Keenan Wynn · Slim Pickens and introducing Tracy Reed (as "Miss Foreign Affairs")

Screenplay by Stanley Kubrick, Peter George & Terry Southern Based on the book "Red Alert" by Peter George

Stanley Kubrick

DE: I want to tell you something that I think is relevant to what we're talking about... there was one big issue, a super-issue. It's a long story, but I'll just say, we had Joe Loftus and Andy Marshall, at RAND, who were well known. Loftus had been an Air Force intelligence officer for a long time; he worked with the CIA. Andy Marshall, by the way, is still consulting at the Pentagon. He's in his nineties. I'm talking now about '58, that's almost sixty years ago, you see? And he was Rumsfeld's closest advisor. He was a very mysterious figure, and a very close friend of mine at the time. Back then he was at RAND, we knew he had an intelligence clearance, whatever that meant. Actually we knew that he dealt with the CIA. We didn't know that meant anything. Now, in particular, it meant he had a K clearance, a KEYHOLE.

Now, the point about the T[ALENT] and K[EYHOLE] being separated was that nobody knows about the plane. It's only when Khrushchev shoots down a U-2 that people learn about the U-2 program. Before that, before '60, only a handful of people, including some reconnaissance experts in RAND who worked with the U-2, knew there was a U-2. So, the rest of the people at RAND, like, you don't know the names probably, like Albert Wohlstetter, but you may have heard of Herman Kahn.

JC: Yup.

DE: You've seen *Dr. Strangelove*?

ES: No.

JC: Oh my God!

ES: Before my time, man.

DE: Okay, so the words of Dr. Strangelove are largely verbatim quotes from Herman Kahn. He had a Q clearance, so he didn't know. He was in the physics division—for the design of nuclear weapons—a separate clearance. Herman Kahn was famous on thermonuclear war. He was a major model for Dr. Strangelove. Curtis LeMay was General "Buck" Turgidson. Dr. Strangelove from the Bland Corporation is an amalgam of Herman Kahn, particularly the words, and Henry Kissinger . . . And Wernher von Braun, the Nazi, gives the Nazis . . . *Mein Fuhrer! (all laughing)* His arm goes crazy.

JC: I always thought there was a little Edward Teller in there, too.

DE: And Teller is in there, yes, also. So, there are the four guys. Kahn is known to the public as the thermonuclear war man in terms of strategy and supporting, see? He did not have these other clearances. And we were his buddies. He did not know they existed, and neither did Albert Wohlstetter. RAND was, at that point, obsessed, night and day, with the idea that there were more missiles than the CIA was admitting—Soviet missiles—and that there was a missile gap.

And we were working, literally, seventy hours a week, I was there on Sundays, Saturdays, day and night at RAND on the basis that there *was* a missile gap, and the whole building is working on it. *(Pause)* Marshall says, *There is no missile gap.* And he couldn't tell us why, see? We respected Marshall enormously . . . that's why he was there for about fifty years. Very brilliant, he's also quite right wing. And he had another characteristic that I recognized; he was amazingly close mouthed. Not everybody is. One thing is getting the clearance in the first place, but keeping the clearance is another matter, and getting higher clearance is another. And the way you get the higher clearances is when the people who can watch you know, for instance, that you're sitting with your best friend who's saying something wrong, and you could easily correct him—and you don't.

JC: Dan, you said that Marshall said, "There was no missile gap." The ramifications of this statement are hard to imagine.

DE: Marshall is a sphinxlike character. His nickname throughout the bureaucracy in the Pentagon was— who's the guy in *Star Wars*? The gnome . . .

JC: Oh, Yoda. (*Laughter*)

DE: Yoda. His nickname was Yoda. He looked like Yoda, he had kind of a frog face, but he was willing to sit in any meeting or anything, without an expression on his face, and not say anything. He was simply a sphinxlike person, and you don't have to be like that to be in this field, but he was, and that's what made it so all the more significant. I spent all this time leading up to the following simple statement, which is: we still didn't know there was a reconnaissance satellite program, the KEYHOLE program. It remained secret for . . . easily a decade, possibly two decades. Taking pictures from one hundred thousand feet is very impressive, but taken

from one hundred *miles*—which is what they're doing—
is very complicated. So that remained a secret for a long
time. And if you had named any person I've ever known,
the person least likely to break that silence was Andy
Marshall. Remember, it was my field, generally, of how
to keep command of the nuclear forces intact under a
nuclear attack.

They called it then "devolution of authority"—that
was the wording—who is going to actually be running
things if the president's been killed under a nuclear
attack? Well, command is one thing—but who's actually going to push the button? Now that's the point I
want to come to. Let me try to do it and not go on forever here the way I do. . . . The bottom line is that Andy
Marshall . . . this is a very key moment in history—
secret history, not public history. Very few people
understand it. I'm at SAC headquarters, Strategic Air
Command headquarters, in August of '61 to see what
the reaction is to the draft war plan that has just come
to them from McNamara. And the question about the
missile gap is changing their war plans enormously,
radically. The chief of war plans deputy says, "The
question is how many missiles do the Soviets have?"
And he says, "You know what the Old Man thinks?"
The "Old Man" was Thomas Power, who led the raid
on Japan, the one that killed eighty thousand people
in one night.

AR: In Tokyo.

DE: Yes, under LeMay. LeMay wasn't allowed to go.

AR: And McNamara was involved, too?

DE: McNamara had recommended this raid.

AR: Hmm.

DE: He says, the Old Man says the Soviets have a *thousand* missiles. Now the CIA estimate at that time was, if I remember, one hundred and twenty, and State's was higher than CIA's, I think one hundred and sixty, and the air force was saying *hundreds*. That was in August. In September, they completed the satellite coverage.

JC: So, what was the number? What was the real number?

DE: Four.

JC: So, the real number was four?

(*Dan holds up four fingers*)

DE: Four.

OU: In '61.

DE: In '61. Four intercontinental missiles.

(*Silence*)

DE: And it was a bad missile, very inaccurate, and very, very vulnerable. If you got over there fast, you could blow this thing over. They had these four missiles, liquid-fueled, thin-skinned missiles sitting on one side in Plesetsk. We had forty Atlases and Titans. They had four.

JC: Jesus Christ. So, the entire Armageddon of the planet was predicated on no one exposing the lie that there were only four goddamn missiles.

DE: Yeah . . . but here's a little technical point that I wanted to make. There is a big difference between our assessments of the Soviets having either one thousand missiles, or one hundred and twenty missiles—the one thousand is two hundred and fifty times what they actually had. One hundred and twenty is thirty times the number they actually had. So that's very, very significant. I went back and I told this to RAND at a top-secret briefing. Everybody had to be signed in, all the department heads were there. Herman Kahn used to say, "You must always have a chart in a briefing." I never used charts. Everybody knows that I don't use charts. This time I decided to make some charts. So, here are my charts. There were guards at the door, which you didn't do in the Pentagon. My first chart—John, what was the name of the child in the Santa Claus letter?

JC: Virginia. "Yes, Virginia, there is a Santa Claus ..."

(*Pause*)

DE: So my first chart said—*Yes, Virginia, there is a missile gap.*

(*Laughter*)

DE: The second one said—*It is currently running ten to one.* No reaction. The third said: *In our favor.* As I said we had forty Atlases and Titans, four Soviet ICBMs [intercontinental ballistic missile], and then I went through the rest of them. We had Polaris submarines, we had IRBMs [intermediate-range ballistic missile], we had something like two thousand bombers, strategic bombers, and one thousand tactical bombers in range of the Soviet Union, the Russians had one hundred and ninety-two.

ES: People forget how massive the American industrial advantage was after World War II.

DE: Yeah, but this wasn't just industrial, you see. They hadn't built anything. We thought the Soviets must want the capability to have a first-strike capability against us.

"We had something like two thousand bombers, strategic bombers, and one thousand tactical bombers in range of the Soviet Union, the Russians had one hundred and ninety-two."

We would bend every effort to get that capability if we were them. We estimate they must have it! *So they neither had a first-strike capability nor were they going to have a first-strike capability, nor had they tried to have a first-strike capability.*

Our best first strike, then and now, has never, for a moment—since the mid-'50s—never been able to keep the Soviets from annihilating every last person in West Europe.

By the way, you know we were going to kill—depending on how the wind blew—which depends on the season . . . our private, top-secret estimates were that we would kill every European, a hundred million Europeans, without a single US or Soviet warhead landing on West Europe. Just from the fallout of the attacks we were planning on Russia and East Europe. One hundred million depending on . . .

ES: How the wind blows west across Europe?

DE: Yes.

JC: So the blast radius . . . Dan, tell them about the calculation of fire and smoke . . . the state secret.

DE: Yes, their damage calculations . . . okay, hold on to your socks . . . *they don't calculate the fire and the smoke* . . . only blast and radiation. And fallout . . . because you could calculate those quite accurately. That was their excuse. Their excuse was we can't calculate fire. . . . It's fire that kills most people—but they left that out of their calculations.

JC: So it just doesn't exist.

DE: So ignore it, ignore it, the reality. Fire is the main effect of thermonuclear weapons . . . *to this day* they do not calculate the fire. So they didn't have to ask the question "What about the smoke?" Finally in '83 somebody calculated the effect of just one of these things . . . what 150,000 tons of smoke and soot would cause, lofted into the stratosphere, reducing sunlight for a decade . . . basically it's nuclear famine . . . crops die, livestock dies . . . everybody dies. With a small war between India and Pakistan, fifty Hiroshima-size bombs each, smoke would reduce sunlight enough to starve two billion people to death . . . In a US-Russian war—it's nuclear winter. I never understand why we worry so much about climate change and not about nuclear war. Both have the potential of annihilating life on earth.

AR: Nuclear bombs are the logical corollary to the idea of the nation-state . . . no?

Notes

Things That Can and Cannot Be Said

1. "Field Notes on Democracy: A Conversation with Arundhati Roy," Lannan Foundation in Pursuit of Cultural Freedom lecture series, Thorne Auditorium, Northwestern Law School, Chicago, Illinois, March 18, 2013. Available online at: http://wearemany.org/v/2015/08/field-notes-on-democracy.

2. Richard Seddon, *Philosophy as an Approach to the Spirit: An Introduction to the Fundamental Works of Rudolf Steiner* (East Sussex: Temple Lodge Press, 2005), 28.

3. For information on Freedom of the Press Foundation, visit: https://freedom.press.

4. See James Bamford, "The Most Wanted Man in the World," *Wired*, September 2014. Available online at: http://www.wired.com/2014/08/edward-snowden/.

5. Press Trust of India, "India a Natural Ally of US in Fight Against Terrorism: Walter Russel Mead," August 26, 2013.

6. See, among other historical accounts, David Cortright, *Soldiers in Revolt: GI Resistance During the Vietnam War* (Chicago: Haymarket Books, 2005), with a foreword by Howard Zinn.

7. In 1996, Madeleine Albright, then the US ambassador to the United Nations, was asked on national television what she felt about the fact that 500,000 Iraqi children had died as a result of US economic sanctions. She replied that it was "a very hard choice," but that all things considered, "we think the price is worth it." From Leslie Stahl, "Punishing Saddam," produced by Catherine Olian, CBS, *60 Minutes*, May 12, 1996. For analysis, see Anthony Arnove, *Iraq: The Logic of Withdrawal* (New York: Metropolitan Books, 2007).

8. See Jeremy Scahill, *Dirty Wars: The World Is a Battlefield* (New York: Nation Books, 2013) and Nick Turse, *The Changing Face of Empire: Special Ops, Drones, Spies, Proxy Fighters, Secret Bases, and Cyber Warfare* (Chicago: Haymarket Books, 2012).

9. See Arundhati Roy, *Field Notes on Democracy: Listening to Grasshoppers* (Chicago: Haymarket Books, 2009) and Arundhati Roy, *Capitalism: A Ghost Story* (Chicago: Haymarket Books, 2014).

10. See Arundhati Roy, "The End of Imagination," in *The End of Imagination* (Chicago: Haymarket Books, 2016).

11. See Eqbal Ahmad, *Terrorism: Theirs and Ours* (New York: Seven Stories Press, 2001).

12. See Sharon Smith, "Using Women's Rights to Sell Washington's War," *International Socialist Review* 21 (January–February 2002). Available online at: http://isreview.org/issues/21/afghan_women.shtml. See also Malalai Joya, *A Woman Among Warlords: The Extraordinary Story of an Afghan Who Dared to Raise Her Voice* (New York: Scribner, 2009).

13. Arundhati Roy, *Walking with the Comrades* (New York: Penguin Books, 2011).

14. For an important analysis of Kashmir, see Sanjay Kak, ed., *Until My Freedom Has Come: The New Intifada in Kashmir* (Chicago: Haymarket Books, 2013). Also see Arundhati Roy, "Listening to Grasshoppers: Genocide,

Denial, and Celebration," chapter 9 in *Field Notes on Democracy* (Chicago: Haymarket, 2009) and Arundhati Roy, "Kashmir's Fruits of Discord," op-ed, *New York Times*, November 8, 2010. Available online at: http://www.nytimes.com/2010/11/09/opinion/09roy.html?_r=1

15. On Modi's role in the 2002 Gujarat massacre, see Roy, "Democracy: Who's She When She's at Home?" in *Field Notes on Democracy*, 30–49.

16. "The Oriental doesn't put the same high price on life as does a Westerner," William Westmoreland said. "We value life and human dignity. They don't care about life and human dignity." Quoted in Peter Davis, director, *Hearts and Minds* (Criterion Collection, 1974), 112 minutes.

17. See Howard Zinn, *The Bomb* (San Francisco: City Lights Books / Open Media Series, 2010), 42 and 58.

18. Robert McNamara, interviewed by Errol Morris in *The Fog of War: Eleven Lessons from the Life of Robert S. McNamara* (Sony Pictures, 2004), 95 minutes. Transcript available online at: www.errolmorris.com/film/fow_transcript.html.

"We Brought You the Promise of the Future, but Our Tongue Stammered and Barked . . ."

1. John Cusack, "The Snowden Principle," *Huffington Post*, June 14, 2014. Available online at: www.huffingtonpost.com/john-cusack/snowden-principle_b_3441237.html. Cusack writes, "At the heart of Edward Snowden's decision to expose the NSA's massive phone and Internet spying programs was a fundamental belief in the people's right-to-know. 'My sole motive is to inform the public as to that which is done in their name and that which is done against them,' he said in an interview with the *Guardian*. From the State's point of view, he's committed a

crime. From his point of view, and the view of many others, he has sacrificed for the greater good because he knows people have the right to know what the government is doing in their name. And legal, or not, he saw what the government was doing as a crime against the people and our rights. For the sake of argument—this should be called The Snowden Principle."

2. Daniel Ellsberg, *Secrets: A Memoir of Vietnam and the Pentagon Papers* (New York: Viking, 2002).

3. Ibid., 68.

4. Ibid., 66.

5. Ibid., 68–69.

6. Nick Turse, *Kill Anything That Moves: The Real American War in Vietnam* (New York: Metropolitan Books, 2013.)

7. In addition to Turse, *Kill Anything That Moves*, see Noam Chomsky, *At War with Asia: Essays on Indochina* (Oakland: AK Press, 2004).

8. Ellsberg, *Secrets*, 72.

9. For one instructive account, see Nigel Harris, *The Mandate of Heaven: Marx and Mao in Modern China* (Chicago: Haymarket Books / IS Books, 2015).

10. Nicholas Kristof, "Bill and Melinda Gates's Pillow Talk," *New York Times,* July 19, 2015. Available online at: www.nytimes.com/2015/07/19/opinion /sunday/nicholas-kristof-bill-and-melinda-gatess -pillow-talk.html.

11. John Oliver, interview with Edward Snowden, *Last Week Tonight, HBO,* April 5, 2015. Available online at: www.youtube.com/watch?time_continue =1217&v=XEVlyP4_11M.

12. Varlam Shalamov, *Kolyma Tales* (New York: Penguin Classics, 1995.

13. Anna Akhmatova, "Instead of a Preface," in Roberta Reeder, ed., *The Complete Poems of Anna Akhmatova,* expanded ed. (Edinburgh: Canongate, 1997), 384. Translation by Judith Hemschemeyer.

14. See J. M. Coetzee, "Osip Mandelstam and the Stalin Ode," *Representations* 35 (Summer, 1991), 72–83.

15. Arthur Koestler, *Darkness at Noon: A Novel* (New York: Scribner, 2006).

16. Ibid., 59.

Things That Can and Cannot Be Said (Continued)

1. "Irked by Atom Test Protestors, Soviet Hauls Them Out to Sea," *New York Times*, June 4, 1982.

2. B. R. Ambedkar, *Annihilation of Caste: The Annotated Critical Edition*, introduction by Arundhati Roy (New York: Verso Books, 2014).

3. The Right Livelihood Award Ceremony, December 1, 2014. Available online at: www.youtube.com /watch?v=LJDhzTzXzu8. For additional details, visit: www.rightlivelihood.org/snowden.html. "Snowden's revelations have caused a worldwide reevaluation of the meaning of privacy and the boundaries of rights," the committee noted in its commendation.

4. See Arundhati Roy, "Confronting Empire," *Outlook (India)*, January 30, 2003. Available online at: www .outlookindia.com/article/confronting-empire /218738. See also Arundhati Roy, *The End of Imagination* (Chicago: Haymarket Books, 2016).

5. See "Arundhati Roy Addresses Tens of Thousands at World Social Forum Opening in Bombay," *Democracy Now!* January 20, 2004. Available online at: www. democracynow.org/2004/1/20/arundhati_roy_ad- dresses_tens_of_thousands.

6. See, among other sources, Robert Arnove, ed., *Philan- thropy and Cultural Imperialism: The Foundations at Home and Abroad* (Bloomington: Indiana Univer- sity Press, 1982) and Joan Roelofs, *Foundations and Public Policy: The Mask of Pluralism* (Albany: State University of New York Press, 2003). On Indonesia, see Edward S. Herman and Noam Chomsky, *The Washington Connection and Third World Fascism: The Political Economy of Human Rights—Volume I*

(Chicago: Haymarket Books, 2015) and *After the Cataclysm: Postwar Indochina and the Reconstruction of Imperial Ideology: The Political Economy of Human Rights—Volume II* (Chicago: Haymarket Books, 2015).

7. Joshua Oppenheimer, director, *The Act of Killing* (Cinedigm, 2013), 123 minutes.

8. See Laurence H. Shoup and William Minter, *Imperial Brain Trust: The Council on Foreign Relations and United States Foreign Policy* (New York: Monthly Review Press, 1977).

9. Roy, *Capitalism: A Ghost Story*, 24.

10. Noam Chomsky, *For Reasons of State* (New York: New Press, 2003), with a foreword by Arundhati Roy.

11. Ibid., 3–4.

12. Julian Assange, *When Google Met WikiLeaks* (New York: OR Books, 2014).

13. See Nakul Singh Sawhney, *Muzaffarnagar Baaqi Hai [Muzaffarnagar Eventually]* (2015), 136 minutes.

14. John Elliott, "India's Modi Merges Myth and Reality," *Asia Sentinel*, October 31, 2014. Available online at: www.asiasentinel.com/politics/india-modi -merges-myth-and-reality/.

15. See Modris Eksteins, *The Rites of Spring: The Great War and the Birth of the Modern Age* (New York: Mariner Books, 2000), 304.

16. Roy, *Walking with the Comrades*, 52.

17. Ibid., 51.

18. Ibid., 51.

19. "The Doctor and the Saint" is the title of Arundhati Roy's introduction to B. R. Ambedkar, *Annihilation of Caste.*

20. Roy, *End of Imagination*, 54.

21. Edward Everett Hale, "The Man Without a Country." Available online at: www.bartleby.com/310/6/1.html.

22. Sir Walter Scott, "Patriotism." Available online at http://bartleby.com/101/547.html.

23. Afterward, as Siddhartha Deb notes, "Arundhati Roy was issued a criminal contempt notice by a Nagpur court, for an article she published in *Outlook* magazine about G. N. Saibaba, a disabled political dissident

confined to a wheelchair, who had been awaiting trial for a year. Roy argued Saibaba should not be prevented from getting bail if Bajrangi and Kodnani, convicted for their role in the 2002 massacres, could, and if Amit Shah, once charged with ordering extrajudicial executions, functioned with impunity as president of the BJP 'and the right-hand man of Prime Minister Narendra Modi.'" (Deb, "Unmasking Modi," *New Republic*, May 3, 2016.) See also Roy's own account of these developments in her essay "My Seditious Heart: An Unfinished Diary of Nowadays," in *The End of Imagination*.

What Shall We Love?

1. For context, see Glenn Greenwald, *No Place to Hide: Edward Snowden, the NSA, and the U.S. Surveillance State* (New York: Metropolitan Books, 2014). See also William M. Arkin, *Code Names: Deciphering U.S. Military Plans, Programs, and Operations in the 9/11 World* (Hanover, NH: Steerforth Press, 2005).
2. See Jeremy Scahill and the staff of *The Intercept*, *The Assassination Complex: Inside the Government's Secret Drone Warfare Program* (New York, Simon and Shuster, 2016).
3. Olivia B. Waxman, "Here's How Edward Snowden Was Welcomed on Twitter," *Time*, September 29, 2015. Available online at: http://time.com/4054441/edward-snowden-twitter/. Snowden's Twitter account can be found at: https://twitter.com/Snowden.
4. "WikiLeaks Issues Call for $100,000 Bounty on Monster Trade Treaty," WikiLeaks, June 2, 2015. Available at: https://wikileaks.org/WikiLeaks-issues-call-for-100-000.html and "WikiLeaks Launches Campaign to Offer $100,000 'Bounty' for Leaked Drafts of Secret TPP Chapters," *Democracy Now!* June 2, 2015. Available online at: www.democracynow.org/2015/6/2/wikileaks_launches_campaign_to_offer_100.

Index

About Haymarket Books

Haymarket Books is a nonprofit, progressive book distributor and publisher, a project of the Center for Economic Research and Social Change. We believe that activists need to take ideas, history, and politics into the many struggles for social justice today. Learning the lessons of past victories, as well as defeats, can arm a new generation of fighters for a better world. As Karl Marx said, "The philosophers have merely interpreted the world; the point however is to change it."

We take inspiration and courage from our namesakes, the Haymarket Martyrs, who gave their lives fighting for a better world. Their 1886 struggle for the eight-hour day, which gave us May Day, the international workers' holiday, reminds workers around the world that ordinary people can organize and struggle for their own liberation. These struggles continue today across the globe—struggles against oppression, exploitation, hunger, and poverty.

It was August Spies, one of the Martyrs who was targeted for being an immigrant and an anarchist, who predicted the battles being fought to this day. "If you think that by hanging us you can stamp out the labor movement," Spies told the judge, "then hang us. Here you will tread upon a spark, but here, and there, and behind you, and in front of you, and everywhere, the flames will blaze up. It is a subterranean fire. You cannot put it out. The ground is on fire upon which you stand."

We could not succeed in our publishing efforts without the generous financial support of our readers. Many people contribute to our project through the Haymarket Sustainers program, where donors receive free books in return for their monetary support. If you would like to be a part of this program, please contact us at info@haymarketbooks.org.

Also by Arundhati Roy

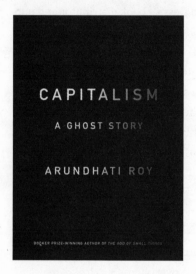

Capitalism: A Ghost Story examines the dark side of democracy in contemporary India, and shows how the demands of globalized capitalism have subjugated billions of people to the highest and most intense forms of racism and exploitation.

Field Notes on Democracy tracks the fault lines that threaten to destroy India's precarious democracy and send shockwaves through the region and beyond.

The End of Imagination brings together five of Arundhati Roy's acclaimed books of essays into one comprehensive volume for the first time and features a new introduction by the author.